JATAKA TALES SERIES

The Value of Friends

Illustrated by Eric Meller

DHARMA  PUBLISHING

Dedicated to
All the World's Children

Endpapers by Margie Horton

Printed in the United States of America by Dharma Press,
1241 21st Street, Oakland, California 94607

Library of Congress Cataloging in Publication Data
will be found at the end of this book.

The Jataka Tales

The Jataka Tales celebrate the power of action motivated by compassion, love, wisdom, and kindness. They teach that all we think and do profoundly affects the quality of our lives. Selfish words and deeds bring suffering to us and to those around us. Selfless actions give rise to goodness of such power that its influence spreads in ever-widening circles, uplifting all forms of life.

The Jataka Tales, first related by the Buddha over two thousand years ago, bring to light his many lifetimes of positive action practiced for the sake of the world. As an embodiment of great compassion, the Awakened One reappears in many forms, in many times and places, to ease the suffering of living beings. Thus the Jataka stories are filled with heroes of all kinds, each demonstrating that compassion and wisdom have the power to transform any situation.

Although based on traditional accounts, the stories in the Jataka Tales Series have been adapted for children of today. May these tales inspire the positive thoughts and actions that will sustain the heart of goodness and illuminate the wisdom of all spiritual traditions for the well-being of future generations.

Tarthang Tulku   Founder, Dharma Publishing

Once upon a time, upon the shores of a peaceful lake in the midst of a forest, there lived a Lion (king of the beasts), an Osprey (king of the birds), and two Hawks. In the middle of the lake was an island, and on this island lived a large tortoise.

One day the gentleman Hawk asked the lady Hawk to be his wife. "Have you any friends?" she asked. "No, my dearest," he replied, "I do not." "Friends are important," she said, "I will marry you, but first you must find some friends. We will need someone who can help us if difficulty and danger arise."

"I wonder who would make the best friends," pondered the Hawk. The lady Hawk responded, "I suggest King Osprey, who lives on the eastern shore, King Lion who lives in the fields to the north, and the great Tortoise who dwells on the island in the middle of the lake."

The Hawk took her advice, and the four animals became firm friends.

For their new
home, the Hawks chose a large flowering tree on
one of the lake's many islands. There among the
branches they made their nest. Before long, the
lady Hawk laid two eggs, and soon two baby
Hawks emerged from the eggs.

One day, some country folk came to the forest hunting for food. Finding nothing, they went to the lake hoping at least to catch a few fish. They went out to an island, and lay down under a great tree to rest for a time, directly below the Hawks' nest. But soon they were bothered by swarms of mosquitoes. To drive the mosquitoes away, they kindled a fire that made clouds of smoke.

The smoke rose up through the tree, making the young birds cough and cry out. "I hear baby birds in that tree," said one of the men. "Quick, make the fire bigger. We will smoke them out, and have those birds for supper." They laid more wood on the fire, and the smoke became very thick. Seeing this, the mother Hawk said to her mate, " Go, my husband, tell the Osprey that our children are in danger."

The Hawk flew as fast as he could to King
Osprey, who was just settling down for the night.
"What is your need, my friend?" asked the
Osprey. "O chief of birds," said the Hawk,

"To the lake the country folk came
hoping to fill their bags with game.
They built a fire under our tree
to catch our young, who cannot flee.
O best of birds, O good friend thou,
gladden our hearts, and help us now."

"Fear not," said the Osprey, "I will come. Go now, and tell your wife:

"In all times and places, those who are wise have friends and companions to protect them. For you, O Hawk, I will perform this deed. Good friends help each other in their need."

Flying to the island, the Osprey saw the men climbing the flowering tree. The king of birds dove into the lake and drenched his feathers with water. Instantly he sprang out again, and flapped the water from his wings into the fire. The fire sputtered and went out. But the men climbed down and made another fire, then returned to the tree. Again the Osprey dove into the lake, and again he put out the fire.

Over and over, the men rebuilt their fire, and again and again the Osprey showered it with water. Finally, seeing the Osprey was tiring, the mother Hawk spoke to her husband again. "My dearest, ask the Tortoise to come so our friend the Osprey can rest."

Immediately, the Hawk flew off, and found the
Tortoise asleep. "What is your errand, friend?"
the awakened Tortoise asked. "Our children are
in great danger. The Osprey has helped, but now
he is very tired. This is why I have come:

"Even they who suffer from doing selfish deeds
    may feel light again if they get help in need.
Our young ones are in danger, so I fly to thee!
O kind lake-dweller — please do help me!"

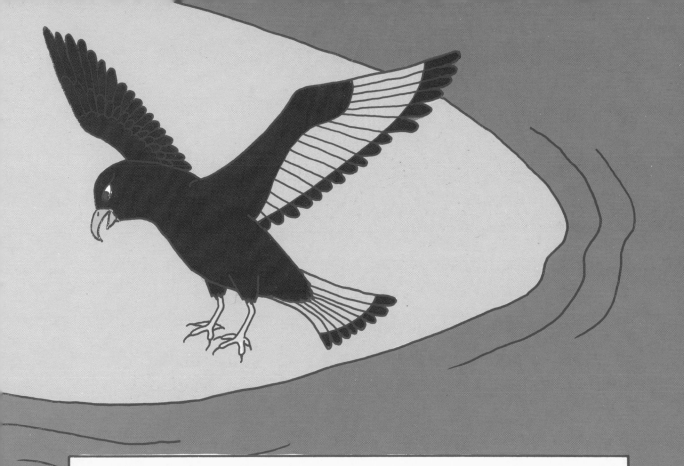

Upon hearing this, the Tortoise replied,

"Those who are generous and kind will lend
food, shelter, even their lives to a friend.
For thee, O Hawk, I will perform this deed!
The good must help each other in their need."

Swimming to the bottom of the lake, the Tortoise
swept up all the mud he could carry. When he
reached the island, he pushed it into the fire, and
the fire immediately went out. Then he pulled
his head and feet into his shell, and lay very
still. The country folk saw him and cried, "Why
should we work so hard to catch a few small
birds? We can just roll this Tortoise over, and
have him for supper instead!"

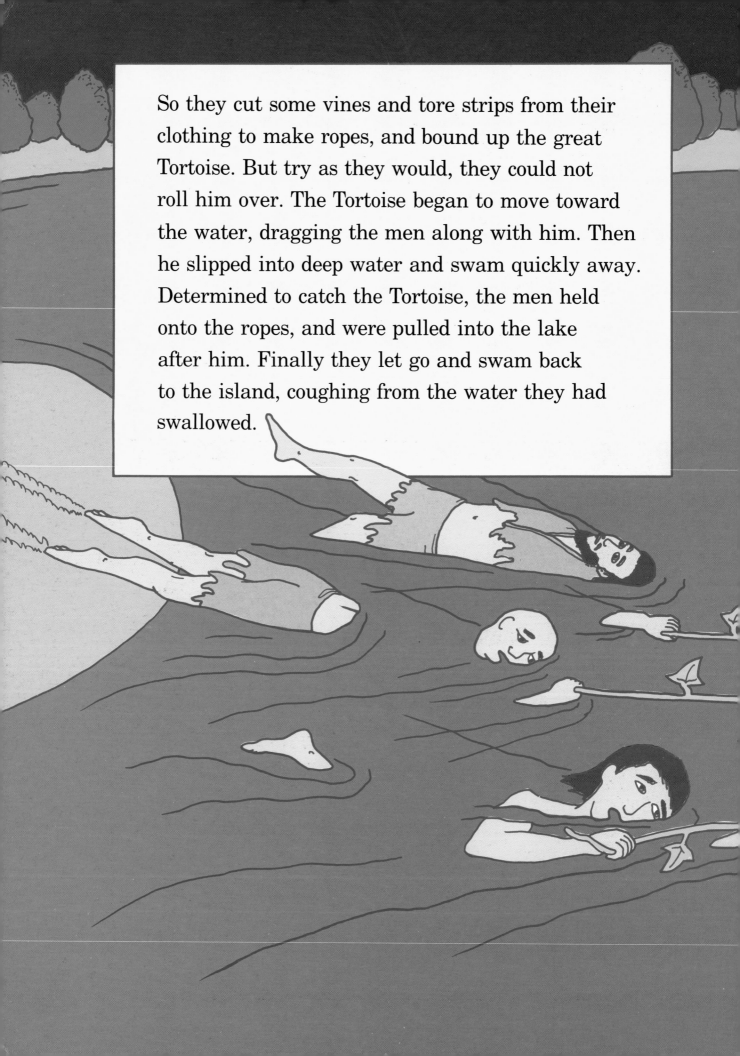

So they cut some vines and tore strips from their
clothing to make ropes, and bound up the great
Tortoise. But try as they would, they could not
roll him over. The Tortoise began to move toward
the water, dragging the men along with him. Then
he slipped into deep water and swam quickly away.
Determined to catch the Tortoise, the men held
onto the ropes, and were pulled into the lake
after him. Finally they let go and swam back
to the island, coughing from the water they had
swallowed.

"What is happening?" they said to each other. "That Osprey kept putting out our fire, then this Tortoise dragged us into the water and tried to drown us. And we still have not eaten! Let's light another fire and catch those young hawks. A few birds are better than no food at all!" The mother bird heard what they said and told her husband, "Sooner or later these men will harm our children. Go now and tell our friend the Lion."

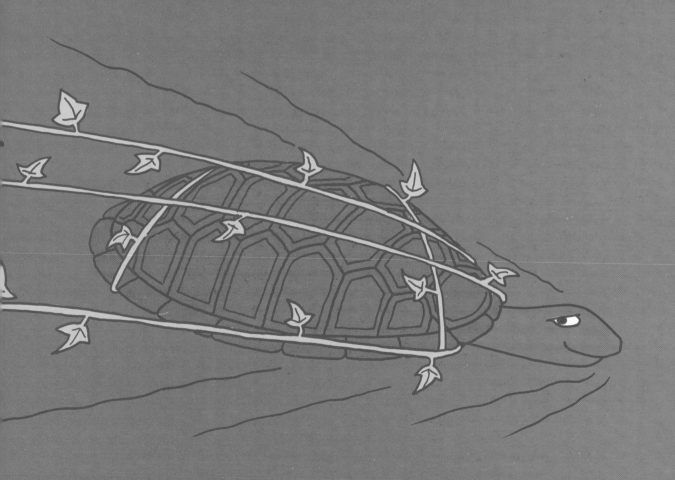

At once the Hawk flew to the Lion, who asked, "Hawk, the sun has not yet risen. Why have you come at this time?" Then the Hawk told him all that had happened.

"Mightiest of beasts, both animals and men
fly to the strongest when they have great fear.
My young ones are in danger; help me, friend!
You are our king, that is why I am here."

The Lion stretched and gave a great roar.

"Yes, I will do what you ask, my friend.
Let us go and put your fear to an end."

The men, seeing a Lion swimming toward the
island, were frightened nearly to death. "The
Osprey put out our fire. The Tortoise made us
ruin our clothes and got us all wet. But now we
are done for! This Lion will destroy us completely!"
In their panic they ran this way and that.

By the time the Lion reached the tree, the men had all disappeared. Then the Osprey, the Hawk, and the Tortoise joined the Lion, and together they celebrated their victory. The Lion praised the value of friends and told them, "Always respect the bonds of friendship. Take care to make good friends you can trust, and respond to their needs with a generous, loving heart." Then each of the friends returned to his own home.

The mother Hawk, looking upon her young ones, thought "How wonderful! Through friendship my children have been saved." To her husband she sang,

"O Hawk, see what making friends has meant!
Thanks to these good friends you sent,
each one of us is safe and sound.
What better help could ever be found?"

And all four friends remained faithful to each other for the rest of their lives.

Colored by _____

My page

Colored by _____

Library of Congress Cataloging in Publication Data

The value of friends.

(Jataka tales series)
Summary: A hawk and his family are made aware of
the value of friendship when their friends the osprey,
the lion, and the tortoise save them from hungry
country folk.

1. Jataka stories, English. [1. Jataka stories]
I. Meller, Eric, ill. 2. Series.
BQ1462.E5V35 1986   294.3'823   86–24164
ISBN 0–89800–154–4
ISBN 0–89800–140–4 (pbk.)